MONSTER ENGLISH

Christabell
HOBBIES	Playing games on her laptop computer
SKILL	Technology whizz
FAVOURITE COLOURS	Pink and red
LIVES	Smile Street with Ezzo, Waldo and Whiffy

Ezzo
HOBBIES	Kung fu
STRENGTH	Martial Arts expert
BEST MOVE	Karate kick
FAVOURITE FILMS	Monster action films

Waldo
FAVOURITE FOOD	Dog biscuits
HOBBIES	Biting squeaky toys
STRANGE FACT	Can change shape
OWNER	Ezzo

Whiffy
FAVOURITE FOOD	Cakes with lots of icing
HOBBIES	Playing, dancing
STRANGE FACT	Turns to invisible vapour when afraid and makes a terrible smell

P (a.k.a. Princess)
HOBBIES	Scheming to take over Monster City
STRENGTH	Deadly scream that knocks everybody out
LIKES	Sparkly things, parties

Edgar
HOBBIES	Making machines to take over Monster City
SKILL	Brilliant scientist
BEST INVENTION	Gripping bow tie
BEST FRIEND	P

Flob
HOBBIES	Monster TV
BEST FRIEND	P won't let him have friends, because she doesn't want any
LIKES	Eating yummy food until his tummy is about to pop

Whiffy grabbed his mouth. "Ow! I bit on something hard!" he exclaimed. The day wasn't starting well. He hadn't even finished breakfast and something bad had happened to him. He fished around inside his mouth and pulled out a small plastic token.

"I'm going to write and complain to the cereal company. They shouldn't let things like this get into their boxes," Whiffy complained. He showed the token to his friends.

"Let me see that cereal packet," Ezzo said and read out the writing on the box: "find a lucky token and win a holiday for you and your friends to Big Fun Beach Holiday Village, for sun, sea and monster good times. Wow, Whiffy! You've won!"

"We're going on holiday! We're going on holiday!" Whiffy chanted and danced excitedly around Christabell and Waldo.

Whiffy loves going on holiday and always purchases new beach shorts. Add the shorts sticker to the picture at the front of the book.

① Suffixes

The cereal company's sensation**al** careless**ness** certainly spoilt Whiffy's enjoy**ment** of his breakfast!

The groups of letters **al**, **ment** and **ness** are all suffixes that are commonly found at the ends of words. Other commonly found suffixes are **ic**, **ary**, **hood** and **ship**.

horrify + ic = horrific

Adding a suffix can sometimes alter the spelling of the root word.

② Word order

Who would have thought that such a small token would turn out to be worth a holiday! Sometimes, even small changes can have a big effect. Take sentences, for example. Changing the order of words can totally them mess up!

I read the book.   I book the read.

On other occasions, a sentence might still make sense after you have changed it, but it means something quite different.

It isn't big.   Isn't it big!

Underline the correct suffix to to make new words.

1 owner hood al ship 8 metal hood ic ship

2 medic al ship hood 9 silly ness ship ment

3 tidy hood ness ic 10 move ic ness ment

4 diction ship ary ic 11 govern ic ment hood

5 history ic hood al 12 fit hood ness ary

6 occasion ship hood al

7 mission al ary ic

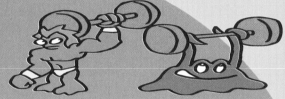

Re-write the sentences so they make sense and tell us about the Smile Street monsters.

1 Whiffy a found token. _____

2 He hurt his token on the tooth. _____

3 Whiffy took the round token to show his friends. _____
_____

4 They realised they won a had holiday. _____
_____

5 'This fantastic is!' said Whiffy. _____

6 Whiffy caused a stink he, because was excited. _____
_____

7 The monsters had to pack what decide they wanted to. _____
_____

8 The monsters will Big Fun Beach at stay. _____
_____

9 The monsters wait for their holiday cannot. _____
_____

10 They are dreaming all of what will do they. _____
_____

11 Sunbathe to wants Christabell. _____

12 Ezzo is forward looking surfing to. _____
_____

The next morning the Smile Street friends were packed and ready to go on holiday. Christabell had a new sunhat and a new waterproof handbag for her laptop computer. Ezzo had trendy new trainers and Whiffy had an amazingly bright new pair of shorts. They all had surfboards. Even Waldo had a special short one made just for him.

"Surf's up!" they cried excitedly as they drove to Monster City Airport.

"We leave from Gate 88," Christabell read the ticket information out loud. "Excuse me. Do you know the way to Gate 88?" she asked a baggage-carrying monster.

"It's in the furthest corner of the airport," he muttered. "You'd better start walking. It takes twenty minutes and there are loads of stairs. Have a nice trip." He was right. It took ages to find the right gate, which was in a shabby, rubbish-strewn corridor.

The Smile Street Gang are keen surfers, even Waldo! Put his surfboard sticker in the right place on the holiday list.

(3) Adjectives

Adjectives describe nouns. They tell us a lot about the things the monsters take on holiday with them.

Adjectives stop stories from being boring. If you choose powerful adjectives, you can make your writing spectacular!

For example, **trendy** trainers are more interesting than **nice** trainers.

Also, "The gate was in a **shabby, rubbish-strewn** corridor."

(4) Prepositions

With their new hats on and Christabell's laptop safely in her new handbag, the monsters head off into the airport to find the departure gate.

The monsters would not get very far without prepositions. These words tell us where one thing is in relation to others – its position.

For example,

Breakfast was **on** the table.

The token was **inside** the cereal packet.

Whiffy danced **around** his friends.

The words in bold are the adjectives.

Waterproof handbag   Trendy trainers   Bright shorts

Can you think up fabulous alternatives to these dreary adjectives?

1 small _____   7 loud _____

2 hungry _____   8 tasty _____

3 dry _____   9 afraid _____

4 hot _____   10 happy _____

5 wet _____   11 funny _____

6 big _____   12 upset _____

Underline the best preposition from the words in bold for these sentences.

1 The departure gate number was printed **on over above inside** the ticket.

2 The gang headed off **under up over across** the airport.

3 The monsters had to climb **through up over along** lots of stairs.

4 Whiffy was nervous about the flight and hid **on under into above** a chair.

5 The baggage-carrying monster shuffled **through under into past** the monsters.

6 Ezzo followed **into above behind on** him to ask if the plane was on time.

7 The monster looked **on in beyond into** a book to check.

8 The monsters' flight number came **down above up below** on the departure board.

9 The Smile Street Gang got ready to go **by under behind through** the gate.

10 Whiffy had gone from under the chair and was hiding **into behind above beyond** a litterbin.

11 "Come **out beyond through down** !" said Christabell.

12 She led him **below towards under into** the departure gate.

Worse was to come when they saw their holiday aeroplane. It had 'Cheapskate Holidays' written on the side.

"Are those bits supposed to hang off?" Whiffy asked worriedly. Things got even more depressing when they finally arrived after a bumpy flight. The Holiday Village turned out to be a couple of tents pitched next to a beach covered in old cans and fish bones.

"Whoever booked this was really mean with their money," Ezzo moaned, kicking a can into the black, oily sea. "Hmm. I think I'll do some checking," Christabell murmured. She set up her laptop and soon found the records for Cheapskate Holidays. The person who booked and paid for this holiday was none other than Edgar!" she announced. "Whiffy, where did you buy that winning box of cereal?" "It was posted to me as a free sample," Whiffy gasped. Christabell slammed her handbag shut. "We'd better get home fast."

Christabell knows that a sunhat is vital to keep a cool head. Pop her hat sticker on the picture.

(5) Contracting words

Now **he's** seen the plane, Whiffy's furious. Taking short cuts with air safety **isn't** on, but it can save time when **you're** writing.

The words in bold are contractions. Contractions are where two words are joined and the missing letters are replaced by an apostrophe. Contractions are used in informal language, like when people speak to one another.

For example,

he has = **he's**

you are = **you're**

(6) Alliteration

Using alliteration, where all the words in a phrase start with the same sound, is a useful way of attracting your reader's attention. You can use it for dramatic effect, humour or to create a particular atmosphere.

For example,

Whiffy's win was woefully weak,

creates a drawn out, sad sound, which reflects how Whiffy feels.

Replace the bold words in Whiffy's letter to Edgar with their shortened, contracted forms.

1   **I am** not happy with my holiday so far. _____

2   It **is not** what was promised on the cereal box. _____

3   I **did not** expect such a long walk to the departure gate. _____

4   I **could not** believe the state of the aeroplane. _____

5   I **would not** fly with you again. _____

6   My friends **will not** either. _____

7   **Ezzo is** furious. _____

8   **He has** never seen such a scruffy plane. _____

9   **He will** get hurt. _____

10 **We have** never had such a bad flight before. _____

11 **It is** outrageous. _____

12 **You are** providing a dreadful service. _____

Can you think of words to fill the gaps in these phrases? Remember, they must use the same sound as the other words in the sentence! Write the words you choose in the spaces.

1   Angry alligators ate _____.

2   Timid tigers taught _____.

3   _____ girls gave gumdrops to Gloria.

4   Sad _____ swam silently to sea.

5   Daring Debbie dived _____.

6   Fearless Fred fed fudge to _____.

7   Teacher Tim tamed _____ toddlers.

8   Mad monkeys made _____.

9   Betty Beale buttered _____.

10 Dainty Daisy _____ down.

11 Jolly Jellyfish _____ joyfully.

12 Loud _____ laugh longest.

"It seems very quiet here," Ezzo remarked when they returned to an empty Monster City Airport. "Too quiet," Christabell replied. "Get ready for trouble."

They made their way through empty city streets. There was nobody about and the only sound was a low rumble. "That reminds me of my Grandad snoring," Whiffy remarked.

"Quick, hide!" Ezzo cried. They all ducked as Flob drove by in a truck. Flob parked the truck and then lumbered into a house. He came back out carrying a sleeping monster under each arm. He did this several times, laying the monsters down in the back of the truck. "That rumbling noise is snoring! The whole town is asleep," Christabell whispered.

"I'd wake up if a big, clumsy idiot like Flob came into my house and carried me out under his slimy arm," Whiffy commented. "Something's wrong," Christabell replied.

Poor Flob! P works him so hard that he needs a holiday too! Add the sun tan lotion in the right place.

7 Plurals

Plurals can be as puzzling as the behaviour of bad monsters. A plural is used when you are describing more than one thing.

Most of the time you just add **s**, or **es** if the word finishes in **s**, **x**, **ch**, or **sh**.

monsters   bush**es**   porch**es**

Words which end in a consonant followed by **y**, end in **ies** when they are made into plurals.

lady   lad**ies**

Some words do not follow the rules, because they stay the same in the plural or have completely different endings!

8 Powerful verbs

The monsters are trying to work out what is going on, but thanks to verbs we know exactly what the characters are doing. Verbs describe actions, such as run, shout, fly.

The monsters are **snoring**.

Flob is **carrying** them to his truck.

Some verbs give you more information than others. A running monster might be jogging slowly or dashing to catch a bus, but a sprinting man is obviously travelling quickly.

Pick the correct plural for each singular noun. Draw a circle around it.

1. holiday → holidaes | holidays | holidayes
2. aeroplane → aeroplane | aeroplanes | aeroplanies
3. hiss → hisss | hisses | hiss
4. box → boxs | boxes | boxies
5. suitcase → suitcases | suitcase | suitcasae
6. child → childs | childes | children
7. salmon → salmons | salmon | salmones
8. baby → babys | babies | babyes
9. mouse → mouses | mouse | mice
10. bus → buss | bus | buses
11. person → people | persones | person
12. nappy → nappyes | nappys | nappies

Can you think of two powerful verbs for each of these words? Write down the words you choose.

1. walk _____ _____   9. hold _____ _____
2. jump _____ _____   10. shout _____ _____
3. eat _____ _____   11. hit _____ _____
4. drink _____ _____   12. laugh _____ _____
5. sleep _____ _____
6. look _____ _____
7. carry _____ _____
8. throw _____ _____

"**Q**uick, jump into the back of the truck," Ezzo urged, as Flob disappeared inside another house. By the time he returned, the four friends were hidden amongst the other monsters and he didn't notice them. He drove to a field on the edge of town, next to P's palace, and began to put his cargo of sleeping monsters down on the grass amongst rows and rows of other monsters, all snoring peacefully.

"Stay hidden," Ezzo whispered to his three friends. They ducked down and Flob drove on to the palace. When they peeped out they saw several bulldozers and diggers lined up in the garden. P and Edgar were there too, studying a roll of plans.

"I want the whole town bulldozed by tomorrow," they heard P insisting. "Then I want to rebuild it my way. I'll start with a P-shaped swimming pool and then I want a P-shaped shopping centre. Everything must be P-shaped."

Ezzo is not at all happy about P's plans, especially as he bought an expensive pair of sunglasses for his trip. Put them on the list.

9 Collective nouns

With everyone in Monster City sleeping like a pile of logs the Smile Street gang have a whole host of problems to deal with.

Sometimes when there is a group of a particular thing, you can use collective nouns to describe them. Pile of logs and host of problems are collective nouns.

a **flock** of sheep

Flock is the collective noun to describe a group of sheep.

10 Prefixes

If P had done her homework, she would know that you do not have to scrap everything and start again when you want to change things. Adding prefixes to the beginning of words can completely change their meaning. A prefix is a collection of letters such as **mis**, **un** and **in**.

Whiffy understood the message on the cereal packet.

Whiffy **mis**understood the message on the cereal packet.

The prefix **mis** added to **understood** changes the meaning completely.

Can you think of commonly used collective nouns for these words? If you can't think of one, make up your own! Write the word in the space.

1 a _____ of cows   7 a _____ of cards

2 a _____ of puppies   8 a _____ of fish

3 a _____ of wolves   9 a _____ of grapes

4 a _____ of lions   10 a _____ of birds

5 a _____ of monkeys   11 a _____ of angels

6 a _____ of flowers   12 a _____ of eggs

Underline the prefixes in these words. Then show P the power of prefixes by writing sentences using the words in the space provided.

1 misplace _____

2 mistake _____

3 misbehave _____

4 non-stop _____

5 non-stick _____

6 nonsense _____

7 exterminate _____

8 export _____

9 exchange _____

10 explode _____

11 co-operate _____

12 coincidence _____

"There's nobody to stop us now I've got those Smile Street idiots out of our hair," Edgar grinned. "By the way, I was thinking of turning Smile Street into a motorway."

"Will it be P-shaped?" P demanded. Edgar's answer was interrupted by a small monster in pink pyjamas rattling the palace gate. "I've just woken up and I can't find anyone," the little monster wailed. "Quick, Flob. Give her some sleeping potion and put her in the field with the others," P ordered.

"I'd better check my potion machinery. If it's running out and more monsters wake up, we'll be in trouble," Edgar frowned. He climbed into the front of Flob's truck, unaware of his enemies hiding in the back. He drove into town, parked and climbed out. The others watched as he stopped by a large, fish-shaped fountain in the city square. He pressed a few hidden buttons to make the fish's mouth flip open automatically.

11 Possessive apostrophes

Apostrophes show what belongs to whom, but not everything belongs to P! When the person or thing an object belongs to is singular, add apostrophe + s.

Ezzo's surfboard.   P's motorway.

When the person or thing an object belongs to is plural, add the apostrophe after the s.

The monsters' surfboards.

12 Common endings

The Smile Street gang have their first clue about P's plans. Words contain clues to help you spell them, too. Often words have common endings. Learning the common endings that lots of words share, can help you to spell new words.

These are common word endings. They will help you to become a super speller and bad monster buster!

light   **station**
serious
special   **tough**

P wants a swimming pool, but Christabell would much rather be swimming in a warm, blue sea. Pop on her swimming costume.

Add apostrophes to the words in bold to show who owns what. Careful, though. Its doesn't have an apostrophe when you are talking about possession. It's is only used instead of it is as a contraction!

1 **Christabells** new handbag is lovely.

2 The **monsters** tail was green.

3 **Whiffys** smell is dreadful.

4 **Ps** plans for Monster City are outrageous.

5 The **baddies** scheme will destroy everything.

6 The **monsters** holiday is making them furious.

7 **Ezzos** patience is running out.

8 **Waldos** shape-changing comes in very handy.

9 P wants to make even the **childrens** playground P-shaped.

10 The baggage-carrying monster took **its** time at the airport.

11 The corridor was covered with rubbish and old **babies** nappies.

12 The departure **gates** hinges squeaked when it opened.

Can you pick the correct spelling for the words in bold? Not all words follow the rules! Underline the words you choose.

1 Christabell's **reacion reaction** to the mystery was as logical as ever.

2 It's **obvious obveus** that P is up to no good.

3 P is **envius envious** of Christabell.

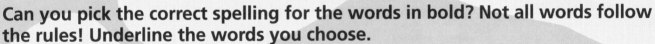

4 The Smile Street friends always try to do the **right rite** thing.

5 Whiffy's smell makes Ezzo **cough coff**.

6 Christabell and Ezzo have **enuff enough** courage to stop the baddies.

7 They have had enough of P's **antisocial antisoshal** behaviour.

8 The monsters had a huge suitcase to take all their **stuff stough** to the airport.

9 Edgar may need an **electrician electrition** to fix his machine.

10 P is in for a **frite fright** if she thinks she can get away with her plan.

11 Destroying Monster City would cause **financial finantial** chaos.

12 If P's plan does not work she will go off in a **hough huff**.

He climbed up the fountain into the mouth and disappeared inside as it closed behind him.

"Let's follow Edgar," Ezzo whispered. They raced over to the fountain and found its hidden control panel. Christabell opened her handbag and plugged her laptop into it.

Random numbers floated up on her screen, as the laptop tried to decode the machine. Finally, a long string of numbers fell into place. Christabell punched them into the fountain's control panel and the fish's head opened up.

As the friends climbed up the side of the fountain, towards the fish head, Waldo stuck out his tongue to lap some water. His eyes shut and he instantly fell asleep! Ezzo grabbed him before he fell. "Edgar must be polluting the city's water supply with a sleeping potion!" Christabell exclaimed. "Sweet dreams," Ezzo whispered and slipped Waldo gently under his arm.

13 Commas

Without punctuation, it would take Christabell's laptop to decode most writing, because all the words would run into one another! Commas are particularly useful, as they tell you where to pause when you are reading sentences and they help you to work out the meaning of a sentence.

You should put commas in where you would naturally take a breath, so it often helps to read the sentences out loud when deciding where to put them.

Edgar, P and Flob planned to put their enemies to sleep, bulldoze the town, then totally rebuild everything. It was a clever, cunning plan.

14 Compound words

Christabell has pieced together the clues and has realised what P and Edgar are up to. Can you be as clever as Christabell and make compound words? Compound words are made up from two or more smaller words.

high + chair = highchair

motor + way = motorway

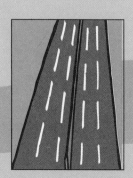

I wonder what Waldo is dreaming about? Building sandcastles on a golden beach perhaps! Add the sticker.

Can you decode these sentences for Christabell by putting in the commas?

1 In the end the baddies will be defeated.

2 Without looking Waldo ran into the road.

3 Unfortunately Whiffy hurt his mouth on the token.

4 He took the token out of his mouth then went to show his friends.

5 The Smile Street friends need more clues then they can defeat P.

6 To get into the fountain Christabell had to use her laptop.

7 Climbing up the fountain Edgar nearly fell.

8 Christabell Ezzo and Waldo climbed up after Edgar.

9 After them Whiffy climbed up.

10 When he gets nervous Whiffy starts to pong.

11 Without knowing where it was going the monsters followed Edgar's truck.

12 P Edgar and Flob do not know the Smile Street friends are back in town.

Match the two word columns to make a compound word. Join them with a line.

1 hand

2 wheel

3 cup

4 rail

5 suit

6 lawn

7 butter

8 farm

9 chair

10 door

11 foot

12 match

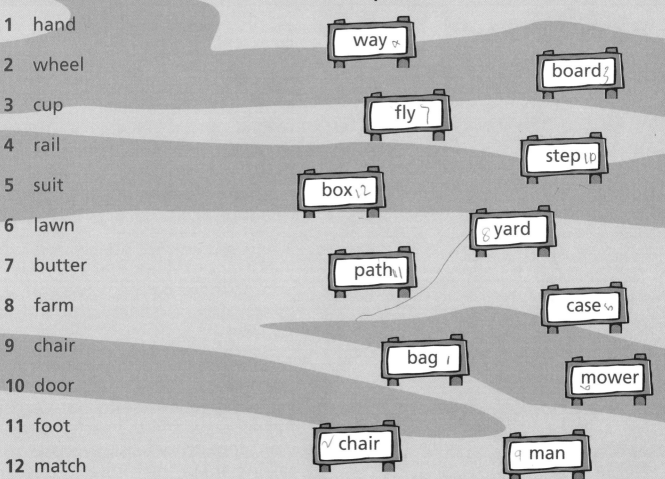

way ∝

board 3

fly 7

step 10

box 12

8 yard

path 11

case 5

bag 1

mower

√ chair

9 man

Inside, a ladder led down into an old tunnel. The damp walls were dripping with slime. Christabell's foot slipped off a ladder rung. One of her boots fell off and tumbled down into the blackness. As it hit the ground the noise echoed around the tunnel walls.

"Do you think Edgar heard that?" Whiffy whispered nervously. Lights came on and an alarm sounded. The fountain slammed shut behind them. "Get down quickly!" Ezzo cried. They raced down into the tunnel, where Christabell grabbed her red boot and slipped it on. "What's that loud clanking noise?" Whiffy wailed.

Three silver robot monsters came around the corner. They had pincers like lobsters and long armoured tails that swished angrily from side to side. Ezzo took an amazing karate leap through the air, slamming his foot into one of the robots. It toppled over and smashed into pieces.

Christabell is wearing her red boots, but she'd much rather be wearing her holiday flip-flops somewhere hot! Pop them on the list.

15 Homophones

The sound of Christabell's boot falling may have alerted Edgar, but you cannot always believe your ears. Some words can sound exactly the same, but be spelt quite differently. They are called homophones.

Ball and bawl sound the same, but mean something very different! Ball is a round thing you kick; bawl is a loud crying noise.

Always look at the sense of the sentence to decide which spelling is the right one and use a dictionary to help you if you need to.

16 Verb endings

All this action called for lots of lovely verbs – action words! The endings of verbs change according to the tense; whether it has happened (the past), is happening now (the present), or will happen (the future).

When you are writing, it is very important to check that you have written in the correct tense and have not flipped backwards and forwards!

Time words give you a clue about the tense you need. The word **yesterday** tells us that what happened was in the past and the word **tomorrow** tells us we are talking about the future.

Here are some homophone pairs. Write a sentence using each word.

1 eight _____

2 ate _____

3 four _____

4 for _____

5 waste _____

6 waist _____

7 hare _____

8 hair _____

9 mail _____

10 male _____

11 see _____

12 sea _____

Past, present or future? Write the word that describes the tense.

1 Edgar invented the sleeping potion yesterday. _____

2 P is showing Flob her plans tomorrow. _____

3 Flob heaved the sleeping monsters out of their houses. _____

4 Then he carried them to the park. _____

5 He is worried about dropping them. _____

6 Ezzo has been spying on the baddies. _____

7 The little monster cried when it woke up. _____

8 Christabell taps the code into the fountain keypad. _____

9 The robots try to attack the Smile Street gang. _____

10 They were hissing and buzzing as they moved. _____

11 Christabell is exploring the tunnels. _____

12 Monster City is relying on the Smile Street gang to save them. _____

eanwhile, Christabell had rummaged in her handbag and pulled out a special wire.

"After you," Ezzo said politely as the remaining two robots marched towards them, waving their pincers.

Christabell jumped on to a robot's back and stuck the wire into its control panel as she held on tightly, riding it like a bucking horse. It flashed and then fell over.

"My turn," Ezzo grinned and karate-chopped the third robot into two halves.

They ran on down the tunnel. Suddenly, sharp metal spikes flew out from the walls, almost trapping Ezzo. He squeezed through them just in time. Then he helped the others to climb through the spaces between the spikes.

They found themselves splashing through cold, murky water.

You never know when you might need waterproofs, which is why Christabell had a special bag made for her laptop. Put it on the picture.

17 Letter strings

Christabell's special wire has saved the day! Letter strings can be useful too. They often make the same sounds in different words, so they can help you find words that rhyme. They also help you to spell new words. They can make different sounds too, so you need to be careful.

Letter strings you will see a lot include:

ss au wa ear ai ice
wo ough ou ight and

18 Similes

Ezzo's reactions are as fast as lightning.

Similes are descriptions that help us to describe things in an interesting way by comparing them with something else.

As bright as a button.

That means a person is clever!

As good as gold.

That means a person is well-behaved!

Add the missing letter strings from the list on the opposite page to these words.

1 _ _ s p   _ _ n t

2 t _ _ _ _   e n _ _ _ _

3 f u _ _   a s s e _ _

4 p o _ _ i b l e   s e _ _ i o n

5 _ _ l f   _ _ m a n

6 m _ _ _ _   t _ _ _ _

7 s _ _ s a g e   b e c _ _ s e

8 c _ _ l d   s h _ _ l d

9 d r _ _ _ y   f _ _ _ _

10 p o l _ _ _   r _ _ _

11 _ _ b b l e   _ _ k

12 p _ _ r   f _ _ r

Complete these monster similes. Be as imaginative as you like!

1 as bold as _____

2 as quiet as _____

3 as blind as _____

4 as brave as _____

5 as green as _____

6 as quick as _____

7 as dry as _____

8 as light as _____

9 as big as _____

10 as fresh as _____

11 as strong as _____

12 as pretty as _____

Around the next bend they saw Edgar. He was standing by a tank of sleeping potion that was dripping slowly into the town's water supply. He was topping it up with new mixture when he spotted the Smile Street crew.

"You should have stayed on holiday," he hissed threateningly.

"We might have done, if you hadn't been too mean to pay for a good one," Christabell replied. "You ruined your own plans!"

"Not quite," Edgar chuckled and pulled a lever. A metal net fell down from the roof above, trapping his enemies.

"Oh, look what I've caught. I'm good at fishing, aren't I?" he giggled. "Now you can all take a holiday down here for a while. I've got a city to flatten. Bye!"

He waved and ran away towards the fountain, leaving them alone and helpless.

Poor Waldo is trapped in evil Edgar's net, when he really wants to be playing with his new beach toy. Add it to the front of the book.

(19) Irregular tense changes

Escaping from Edgar was never going to be simple! Verbs can be tricky too, because some do not follow any of the rules when they change tenses. Usually, to make a verb past tense, we add **ed**.

I am escaping from Edgar becomes I escaped from Edgar. Some verbs are different, though, and all we can do is learn them!

I go becomes **I went**, not I goed!

(20) Double consonants

Edgar wasted no time in trapping the Smile Street buddies so he could flatten Monster City. Spelling words with a double consonant in the middle, like trapping, is easy. If the vowel before the double letters has a short sound, like the **a** in **trapping**, you know the consonant needs to be doubled. But if the vowel makes a long sound, like the **a** in **tape**, the consonant stays single.

As usual, there are some exceptions, particularly words which start with **mod**, like modern. They never have a double consonant.

Do you know the past tense of these tricky verbs? Write the words in the spaces.

1 think _____

2 get _____

3 make _____

4 sit _____

5 hide _____

6 are _____

7 have _____

8 buy _____

9 meet _____

10 sleep _____

11 find _____

12 grow _____

Can you cross out the word in each pair of bold words that is spelt incorrectly?

1 P won't be **hapy happy** until Monster City is destroyed.

2 The Smile Street friends are **hoping hopping** they can stop her.

3 Edgar was **hopping hoping** mad when he found the monsters in the tunnel.

4 Monster City is a very **modern moddern** place.

5 Will the Smile Street monsters be **able abble** to beat the baddies?

6 Flob **hobbled hobled** to the park carrying sleeping monsters.

7 It does not **mater matter** what P does, the Smile Street monsters will beat her.

8 Whiffy has **written writen** a letter of complaint about the holiday.

9 Flob found it hard to **cary carry** the sleeping monsters.

10 Things are **getting geting** serious for Monster City.

11 Ezzo is very good at **running runing**.

12 Whiffy's **leter letter** describes the dreadful holiday village.

Whiffy was so frightened, he was making a terrible smell and had turned invisible, but that couldn't help him escape through the net. Nor could Ezzo's karate kicks or Christabell's gadgets.

"Woof!" A small sound came from under Whiffy's arm. Whiffy's worst smell usually knocked Waldo out, but this time it had woken him up instead! He yawned and shook himself. "Waldo, can you help us escape from this net?" Ezzo asked. Waldo used his special powers to make himself thin and stringy, like a long worm. Then he wriggled through the netting, turned back into his usual shape and ran over to the lever, pushing it up to raise the steel net.

Christabell took a perfume bottle from her handbag, emptied the perfume out and filled the bottle with sleeping potion. Then Ezzo leapt through the air and with a deadly kung fu chop, he smashed the machinery dripping the potion into the water supply.

Ezzo's so annoyed with Edgar's net, he gives a mighty kung fu chop. He'd much rather be using his own net in rock pools!

21 Characters

Clever writers know how to create interesting characters using descriptions of their appearance and behaviour. The paragraphs on this page, for example, describe Whiffy's terrible smell when he feels frightened, Ezzo's deadly karate kicks and kung fu chops, Waldo's incredible shape-changing powers and the useful gadgets Christabell carries in her handbag.

Interesting characters, described in detail, seem 'real' to the person reading the story. Characters who seem real make people want to read stories about them.

22 Suffixes

Waldo's shape-changing skills help the monsters to escape from the net. You can be just as clever by turning nouns and verbs into adjectives by adding suffixes like **able**, **worthy**, **ic** or **ing**.

Waldo is a hero.

His actions are heroic.

hero + ic = heroic

Hero is a noun, but heroic is an adjective. Heroic is the adjective used to describe Waldo's actions.

Can you use what you know about the monsters from the story so far to answer these questions? Write the answers as complete sentences.

1 Who found the winning token in the cereal?
_____

2 Who decided to check up to see who had booked the holiday?
_____

3 Who had booked the holiday?
_____

4 Who "lumbered into a house" to fetch a sleeping monster?
_____

5 Which character likes to collect and analyse information?
_____

6 Who makes a bad smell when he gets scared?
_____

7 Which character can change shape?
_____

8 Who is strong and fast and knows karate?
_____

9 Who can become invisible?
_____

10 In the story for tests 11 and 12, why do you think the little monster wailed when she woke up and could not find anyone?
_____

11 In the story for tests 17 and 18, why did Ezzo smile when he saw the robots?
_____

12 In the story on this page, the goodies destroy the potion machinery. What do you think might happen next?
_____

Pick a suffix from Edgar's net to turn these nouns and verbs into adjectives. Write the new words in the boxes. Be careful, the new spelling isn't always straightforward!

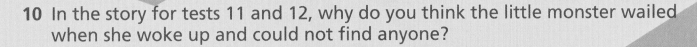

worthy   ly   ful   able
less   ing

1 worth _____   5 hope _____   9 bake _____

2 faith _____   6 trust _____   10 comfort _____

3 beauty _____   7 shake _____   11 harm _____

4 break _____   8 love _____   12 slope _____

They rushed back towards the fountain's mouth, but found it firmly shut. There wasn't even a gap for Waldo to squeeze through. There was a fountain control panel on the wall of the tunnel, but Edgar had smashed it on his way out.

Christabell clicked open her bag and powered-up her laptop. She logged on to the Internet, typed in 'Monster City underground' and soon a map appeared on the screen, showing a tangled mass of different tunnels.

"Wow! That map looks like a bowl of spaghetti," Ezzo remarked.

Christabell led the way back past Edgar's smashed machinery, through one tunnel and then another, navigating by the map. They seemed to be going deeper and deeper underground. Each time they turned in a different direction, the tunnel walls seemed more ancient.

Whiffy's glad his monster lilo doesn't look anything like Edgar. Put Whiffy's lilo on the picture.

23 Setting the scene

The Smile Street friends have found themselves in a tight spot yet again. Good stories carefully describe the setting where the action takes place, so you can really imagine the story happening there. You should always use imaginative descriptions to set the scene when you are writing.

24 Conjunctions

Too many short sentences can leave your writing as complicated as Christabell's map! You can often use conjunctions like **and**, **because**, **then**, **so** or **but** to join two short sentences together. This makes your writing flow better.

Christabell opened her laptop. She looked for a map of the tunnels.

Christabell opened her laptop **and** looked for a map of the tunnels.

They are also useful for joining together two clauses within a sentence, to help explain what is happening.

They needed the map **because** they were lost.

They had the map **so** they could find their way.

Can you use what you know about the inside of the fountain to underline the best description?

1 The inside of the fish's mouth was **gloomy sunny bright**.

2 The ladder led down **steeply gently easily**.

3 The walls of the tunnel were **fresh clean slimy**.

4 The tunnel smelt **like flowers, like chips, musty and damp**.

5 When Christabell's boot dropped to the floor, the sound **echoed sang jingled** around the tunnel walls.

6 The tunnels were like a **maze roadway playground**.

7 The tunnels looked **ancient brand new clean**.

8 When the alarm went off the sound was **muffled deafening quiet**.

9 As Christabell stuck her special wire into the robot **feathers sparks fur** flew.

10 The monsters found themselves **wading swimming flying** through water.

11 The net pinned the monsters down on the **shiny clean dirty** tunnel floor.

12 As the friends reached the fountain mouth they found **a hole it firmly shut a brick wall** facing them.

Can you pick the best conjunction from Christabell's laptop screen to join these sentences together?

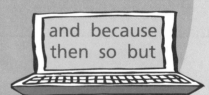

and because
then so but

1 The Smile Street monsters need to escape. They must stop P and Edgar. _____

2 The monsters were asleep. They had drunk Edgar's sleeping potion. _____

3 Ezzo kicked the robot. It fell over. _____

4 Waldo changed shape. He could escape from the net. _____

5 Whiffy smelt terrible. He was very frightened. _____

6 Edgar had smashed the control panel. Ezzo could not use it to escape. _____

7 Waldo tried to find a way out. There were no gaps at all. _____

8 Ezzo smashed the machinery. No more potion could drip into the water. _____

9 Waldo woke up. Whiffy smelt terrible. _____

10 Christabell had her gadgets. They could not help them escape from the net. _____

11 Edgar dropped the net on the monsters. He ran away. _____

12 Christabell's map showed lots of tunnels. Some were very old. _____

At last they crawled out of the musty darkness into the palace garden. The bulldozers and diggers were still parked, ready to destroy the town.

Christabell took out a comb with extra-sharp spikes from her handbag. She used it to puncture the vehicle tyres. Waldo chewed through a few electrical wires and Ezzo unscrewed any screws he could find, until all the building vehicles were useless.

Then Christabell went to find Flob, who was sitting in the field, watching over all the sleeping monsters. "Hello," she said, making him jump. "Y...y...you should be asleep," he stammered, going very red. He secretly liked Christabell, but he had never talked to her before.

"Would you like a drink?" Christabell asked sweetly and handed him her perfume bottle. In no time Flob was asleep, knocked out by the potion in the bottle.

Christabell can't wait until it's their turn to get some rest - sunbathing on a beach! Add their towels to their holiday list.

25 Rhyming words

As our friend Christabell heads for home,
She finds one last job for her comb.
Its sharp teeth cut through rubber tyres,
While Waldo's munch through power wires.

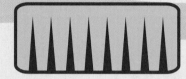

This poem is made up of rhyming couplets, where lines rhyme in pairs. Other poems have different rhyming patterns, and some do not rhyme at all.

26 Speech marks

Poor Flob! He gets in such a state when he sees Christabell, that he can't even talk properly. When a character in a story is speaking, their words are enclosed in speech marks. The story will also say which character is speaking. You will be able to see whether the speech is a question, or an exclamation, from the other punctuation.

"Hello," said Christabell. (Christabell is talking.)

"Stop!" shouted Ezzo. (Ezzo is shouting, so we use an exclamation mark.)

"Where am I?" asked Waldo. (Waldo is asking a question, so we use a question mark.)

Before you can write rhyming poetry, you have to be able to find rhyming words. Can you circle the word from each group that does not rhyme with the word in bold? Careful – sometimes words rhyme even though they are not spelt with the same letter string! Saying them out loud will help you.

1   **rhyme**   rhythm   time   lime   7   **hare**   bear   wear   ear

2   **wrap**   tap   map   tape   8   **cloth**   both   broth   moth

3   **rough**   stuff   cough   enough   9   **meat**   eat   peat   great

4   **bald**   scald   called   told   10   **bored**   scared   lord   scored

5   **far**   fare   are   bar   11   **hour**   scour   pour   flour

6   **stole**   hole   bowl   owl   12   **break**   take   teak   shake

Add the speech marks to these pieces of writing. Don't forget to add commas, exclamation marks or questions marks, too.

1   The exit is this way explained Christabell.

2   How much further asked Whiffy.

3   Quick yelled Ezzo.

4   Woof exclaimed Waldo.

5   Isn't P dreadful said Christabell.

6   Oh D...d...dear stammered Flob.

7   Shut up screamed P.

8   Where is Edgar demanded P.

9   Here I am announced Edgar.

10   Is Flob asleep wondered Whiffy.

11   Yes he is answered Christabell.

12   Let's wake him up suggested Whiffy.

now it was Ezzo's turn to use the perfume bottle. He had noticed P and Edgar busily drawing up their new city plans on a garden table. He climbed a tree and crawled onto a branch above their heads.

"Hey, ugly mugs," he cried and they both looked up, startled.

"Ezzo!" they cried. As they opened their mouths, he poured sleeping potion down on them. Soon they were snoring, too.

The Smile Street friends spent the rest of the night carrying sleeping monsters back to their homes. When everybody woke up the next day, they had no idea what had happened. They never understood why they had bits of grass stuck on their pyjamas and in their hair.

Ezzo and his friends even took Flob and P back to their rooms in the palace, but they left Edgar out in the garden because he'd been so horrible to them.

Ezzo likes heights, which is why he likes surfing the biggest waves. Pop on his surfboard.

(27) Adverbs

Ezzo is always on the move, running quickly from place to place and dealing swiftly with the baddies. Adverbs like **quickly** and **swiftly** tell us more about how Ezzo does things. You can often make adverbs by adding **ly** to an adjective.

Ezzo's running was quick.

He ran **quickly**.

If the adjective already ends in **y**, you need to change the **y** to an **i** before you add **ly**.

P's scream was angry.

She screamed **angrily**.

(28) Alphabetical order

There are so many monsters to take home that Christabell finds a Monster City street map on the Internet to help them. To use the index, the monsters need to be able to put the streets in alphabetical order, even when the first few letters of the street names are the same. If you have several words that start with the same letter, look at the second letter.

Cat and chat both start with a **c**. Cat comes first in alphabetical ordering, because the second letter of cat is **a**, and the second letter of chat is **h**. **a** comes before **h** in the alphabet, so cat comes first.

Change each of these adjectives into adverbs. Then write a short sentence using them.

1 kind _____ _____

2 cross _____ _____

3 slow _____ _____

4 loud _____ _____

5 gloomy _____ _____

6 furious _____ _____

7 sleepy _____ _____

8 tired _____ _____

9 glum _____ _____

10 gentle _____ _____

11 sweet _____ _____

12 peaceful _____ _____

Number these street names from 1–12, starting with the one that comes first in the alphabet. Like where trouble starts in Monster City, they all start with P!

1 Pankhurst Close ☐   7 Palestine Crescent ☐

2 Pannell Way ☐   8 Palingham Gardens ☐

3 Pankridge Road ☐   9 Palace Way ☐

4 Palmer Avenue ☐   10 Palladium View ☐

5 Palewell Park ☐   11 Pampisford Road ☐

6 Pams Way ☐   12 Panmuir Road ☐

P, Edgar and Flob were so knocked out by the potion that they slept for five days.

The Smile Street friends took the opportunity to go on a really good holiday, where the beaches had white sand and the warm, blue waves were perfect for monster surfing.

P was not happy when she eventually woke up and found that everything was not P-shaped after all. She set out to find Edgar and shout at him for ruining her wonderful plan.

Edgar was even less happy when he woke up, still in the palace garden, with an angry P glaring at him.

"I think I need a holiday," he groaned, as a worm curled itself around his bow tie and a slug crawled out of his ear.

Finally, the goodies get to go on a fabulous holiday. Don't forget to add the final sticker - a beach ball for happy holiday fun!

(29) Choosing the best word

The Smile Street friends certainly deserve a brilliant holiday after doing such a fabulous job of stopping the baddies.

Using words like brilliant and fabulous, instead of nice or good, can make your writing much more interesting to read, as long as you don't overdo it. Brilliant is a more powerful word than nice, so it makes your writing more powerful.

(30) Male or female

Lots of words tell us whether the person or animal they are talking about is male or female. Edgar is a **villain** because he is male. P is a **villainess**, which tells us she is female by adding the suffix **ess**.

Sometimes, a completely different word is used to describe male and female. A **fox** is male, but a **vixen** is female.

Some words are gender neutral, so we do not know if the person is male or female from the description. For example, the word **chairperson** is neither male nor female.

Ezzo needs help writing his postcard to Monster City. Cross out the boring words in bold and replace them with more interesting words or phrases.

1 Having a **nice** _____ time.

2 The weather is **hot** _____.

3 The sea is **cold** _____.

4 We are having a **good** _____ time.

5 When we arrived we were all **tired** _____.

6 Christabell has **found** _____ some good places to eat.

7 Whiffy is still making a **bad** _____ smell.

8 Waldo is **angry** _____, because we forgot his surfboard.

9 He **looked** _____ for it in our luggage, but it wasn't there.

10 Christabell **went** _____ straight out to buy him one.

11 Since then he has been **bad** _____ tempered.

12 His tantrums are **funny** _____.

Can you sort these words into male and female forms and come up with the missing equivalents? Put M for male and F for female, then write the alternative in the space.

1 king ___ _____   7 gander ___ _____

2 lioness ___ _____   8 bull ___ _____

3 wife ___ _____   9 ewe ___ _____

4 hen ___ _____   10 widow ___ _____

5 mother ___ _____   11 duke ___ _____

6 princess ___ _____   12 nephew ___ _____

Answers

Test 1 Suffixes
1 ownership
2 medical
3 tidiness
4 dictionary
5 historic
6 occasional
7 missionary
8 metallic
9 silliness
10 movement
11 government
12 fitness

Test 2 Word order
The corrected sentences are:
1 Whiffy found a token.
2 He hurt his tooth on the token.
3 Whiffy took the token round to show his friends.
4 They realised they had won a holiday.
5 'This is fantastic!' said Whiffy.
6 Whiffy caused a stink, because he was excited.
7 The monsters had to decide what they wanted to pack.
8 The monsters will stay at Big Fun Beach.
9 The monsters cannot wait for their holiday.
10 They are all dreaming of what they will do.
11 Christabell wants to sunbathe.
12 Ezzo is looking forward to surfing.

Test 3 Adjectives
Many answers are possible.
Some examples are:
1 tiny
2 starving
3 crumbly
4 sweltering
5 damp
6 huge
7 booming
8 yummy
9 terrified
10 jolly
11 amusing
12 unhappy

Test 4 Prepositions
1 on
2 across
3 up
4 under
5 past
6 behind
7 in
8 up
9 through
10 behind
11 out
12 towards

Test 5 Contracting words
1 I'm
2 isn't
3 didn't
4 couldn't
5 wouldn't
6 won't
7 Ezzo's
8 He's
9 He'll
10 We've
11 It's
12 You're

Test 6 Alliteration
Some examples are:
1 apples
2 tricks
3 giggling
4 Sid
5 downwards
6 ferrets
7 troublesome
8 music
9 bread
10 ducked
11 jostled
12 Larry

Test 7 Plurals
1 holidays
2 aeroplanes
3 hisses
4 boxes
5 suitcases
6 children
7 salmon
8 babies
9 mice
10 buses
11 people
12 nappies

Test 8 Powerful verbs
Some examples are:
1 stroll, amble
2 leap, hurdle
3 scoff, gobble
4 slurp, guzzle
5 snooze, slumber
6 peep, stare
7 haul, lug
8 chuck, hurl
9 grip, clutch
10 yell, holler
11 knock, bang
12 snigger, giggle

Test 9 Collective nouns
Commonly used collective nouns are:
1 a herd of cows
2 a litter of puppies
3 a pack of wolves
4 a pride of lions
5 a troupe of monkeys
6 a bunch of flowers
7 a pack of cards
8 a shoal or a school of fish
9 a bunch of grapes
10 a flock of birds
11 a host of angels
12 a clutch of eggs

Test 10 Prefixes
1 misplace
2 mistake
3 misbehave
4 non-stop
5 non-stick
6 nonsense
7 exterminate
8 export
9 exchange
10 explode
11 co-operate
12 coincidence
Many sentences using these words are possible.

Test 11 Possessive apostrophes
1 Christabell's
2 monster's
3 Whiffy's
4 P's
5 baddies'
6 monsters'
7 Ezzo's
8 Waldo's
9 children's
10 its
11 babies'
12 gate's

Test 12 Common endings
The correct spellings are:
1 reaction
2 obvious
3 envious
4 right
5 cough
6 enough
7 antisocial
8 stuff
9 electrician
10 fright
11 financial
12 huff

Test 13 Commas
1 In the end, the baddies will be defeated.
2 Without looking, Waldo ran into the road.
3 Unfortunately, Whiffy hurt his mouth on the token.
4 He took the token out of his mouth, then went to show his friends.
5 The Smile Street friends need more clues, then they can defeat P.
6 To get into the fountain, Christabell had to use her laptop.
7 Climbing up the fountain, Edgar nearly fell.
8 Christabell, Ezzo and Waldo climbed up after Edgar.
9 After them, Whiffy climbed up.
10 When he gets nervous, Whiffy starts to pong.
11 Without knowing where it was going, the monsters followed Edgar's truck.
12 P, Edgar and Flob do not know the Smile Street friends are back in town.

Test 14 Compound words
1 handbag
2 wheelchair
3 cupboard
4 railway
5 suitcase
6 lawnmower
7 butterfly
8 farmyard
9 chairman
10 doorstep
11 football
12 matchbox

Test 15 Homophones
Many answers are possible.

Test 16 Verb endings
1 past
2 future
3 past
4 past
5 future
6 past
7 past
8 present
9 present
10 past
11 present
12 present